W9-BAT-403

Fact Finders®

ENDANGERED OCEANS

INVESTIGATING OCEANS IN CRISIS

by Jody Sullivan Rake

Content Consultant:
Craig A. Layman, PhD
Department of Applied Ecology
North Carolina State University

CAPSTONE PRESS
a capstone imprint

Fact Finders Books are published by Capstone Press,
1710 Roe Crest Drive, North Mankato, Minnesota 56003
www.capstonepub.com

Library of Congress Cataloging-in-Publication Data
Cataloging-in-Publication Data is on file with the Library of Congress.

ISBN: 978-1-4914-2038-6 (library binding)
ISBN: 978-1-4914-2213-7 (paperback)
ISBN: 978-1-4914-2228-1 (eBook PDF)

Editorial Credits
Abby Colich, editor; Bobbie Nuytten, designer; Gina Kammer, media researcher;
Tori Abraham, production specialist

Photo Credits
Corbis: Collage/Yi Lu, 22, Corbis News/Jeff Haller, 20, Pascal Parrot, 18, San Francisco Chronicle/Paul Chinn, 25, Terra/Stephen Frink, 19; Landov: Kyodo, 17, DPA/CHRISTIAN CHARISIUS, 16; Nature Picture Library: Jordi Chias, 10; Newscom: Kyodo/*, 26; Shutterstock: Actor (top), 28, Alex Mit, 8, Debra James, 4, elic (waves), 7, Fabien Monteil (bottom left), cover, fluke samed (bottom right), cover, fluke samed, 15, Gary Whitton (bottom), 28, Gigi Peis, 24, gladcov (sun), 7, jan kranendonk, 13, Jolanta Wojcicka (left), 21, lakov kalinin (back), cover, lakov kalinin (back), 1, lazyllama (top right), cover, Lebendkulturen.de (algae), 7, mangostock (back), 29, num_skyman, 14, Photoraidz, 5, Piotr Wawrzyniuk (front), 29, Pushish Donhongsa, 6, Rich Carey, 11, Richard Whitcombe (top left), cover, Richard Whitcombe (right), 21, TFoxFoto, 12, vetryanaya_o, 9, Visions of America, 27, Vitoriano Junior, 23

Printed in Canada.
092014   008478FRS15

Table of Contents

CHAPTER 1

The Blue Planet

The oceans are filled with a diverse array of life.

Rocky shores, tropical coral reefs, frigid polar seas, even the black, sunless deep. The ocean is a collection of many **habitats** all bursting with life. Oceans may seem too big and vast to be harmed by anything humans could do. But the effects of human activities are everywhere.

habitat — the natural place and conditions in which a plant or animal lives

FACT

The average depth of the ocean is about 12,400 feet (3,800 meters). Its deepest point is the Marianas Trench in the western Pacific Ocean. The trench is more than 7 miles (11 kilometers) deep. All of Mount Everest, the world's tallest mountain, would fit into the Marianas Trench. The mountain's top would still be more than a mile from the water's surface!

Trash washes up on shores all over the world.

Giant schools of tuna have been reduced to small, isolated groups. Huge heaps of trash cover large areas of ocean. Dazzling coral reefs are becoming gray lumps of rubble. The oceans and all of the life within them are in danger. The oceans formed billions of years ago. But it has taken less than 150 years to change them forever.

Sea of Life — Why Oceans are Needed

Why should anyone care what happens to oceans? People live on dry land. Many live hundreds of miles from the shore. But what affects the oceans affects people too.

People around the world rely on the ocean as a main source for food. About 3 billion people worldwide eat more than 112 billion pounds (51 billion kilograms) of seafood per year. That's 37 pounds (17 kg) per person. Additionally, fisheries and **aquaculture** provide jobs for 540 million people worldwide.

The ocean is Earth's largest source of oxygen. Oxygen is necessary for all life on Earth. Green plants produce oxygen. **Phytoplankton** are one kind of green plant in the ocean. Billions of these one-celled, tiny plants produce half of all the world's oxygen.

.... Fishers unload their catch
at a market in Sam Muk,
Chonbuti, Thailand.

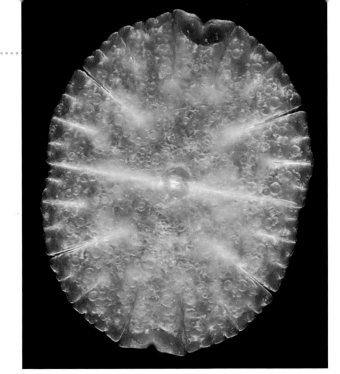

Tiny green plants in the ocean produce most of Earth's oxygen.

aquaculture—raising aquatic animals in water for human use

phytoplankton—different kinds of one-celled organisms that live in water and provide food for larger creatures

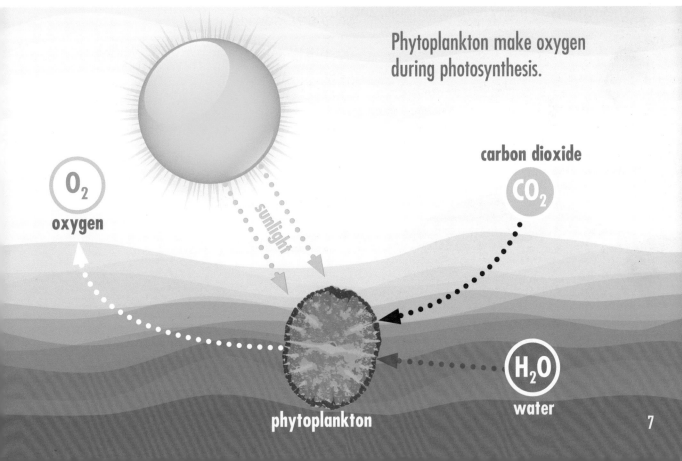

Phytoplankton make oxygen during photosynthesis.

O₂
oxygen

carbon dioxide
CO₂

sunlight

H₂O
water

phytoplankton

Go With the Flow

The oceans play an important role in the weather on land. The sun heats seas near the **equator**. The warmer ocean water moves toward colder seas. This movement, combined with Earth's rotation, creates **currents**. At the same time, water is constantly **evaporating** into the air. This cycle affects weather patterns such as temperature and rain.

Ocean Power

People rely on **fossil fuels** to power homes, cars, and electronics. However, fossil fuels will one day run out. Scientists are researching ways the ocean can provide **hydroelectric** power. The ocean could one day be a source of electricity to many homes, schools, and businesses.

This illustration shows machines that would be able to collect energy from ocean tides.

Water Cycle

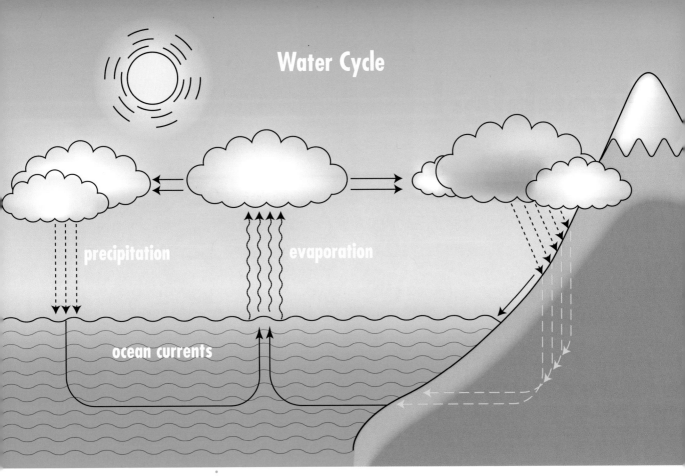

precipitation

evaporation

ocean currents

Water is constantly changing into gas and falling back onto Earth as rain.

equator — an imaginary line around the middle of Earth

current — the movement of water in a river or an ocean

evaporate — to change from a liquid into a vapor or a gas

fossil fuels — fuels, including coal, oil, or natural gas, made from the remains of ancient organisms

hydroelectric — to do with the production of electricity from moving water

CHAPTER 2

Troubled Waters

... a loggerhead turtle trapped in fishing net

Humans have caused major changes to the oceans and the life within them. Countless species are gone forever. Entire habitats are permanently changed. What led the oceans to this troubled state?

What a Dump

Humans have created many things that enhance life on Earth. As different industries grow, harmful amounts of waste and trash increase. This waste and trash are often thrown away in ocean waters. **Pollution** can be anything from a single gum wrapper to tons of toxic waste. Throughout the last decades, ocean pollution has become deadly and permanent.

pollution—harmful materials that damage the air, water, and soil

Pacific Trash

In ocean waters between California and Hawaii, a current spins in a clockwise spiral. For years tons of trash have drifted into this current and become stuck. This area, called the Pacific Garbage Patch, is about the size of Texas. Because it is so far from any country, none have taken responsibility for the cleanup. Several scientists, however, are committed to keeping the trash heap from growing larger.

Solid Waste

Even trash that starts out on land can make its way to the ocean. Litter is now washing up on the coastlines of Antarctica, far from human life. Ocean trash is a double threat to life under the sea. Many animals swallow bits of trash thinking it is food. This causes painful and deadly damage to their bodies. Other times creatures become entangled in lost fishing lines and nets. The lines cut into their flesh and cause terrible gashes. Air-breathing animals, such as dolphins or sea turtles, can drown if they become caught in these nets.

plastic litter floating in the ocean

The Many Pollution Sources

Other kinds of ocean pollution cannot be easily seen. **Nonpoint source pollution** doesn't come from any one source. It comes from a bunch of small ones. These include homes, farms, and vehicles. When people wash their cars, the soap rinses off into a drain. The drain may run into a nearby river. It eventually reaches the ocean. When farmers plant their crops, some of the **fertilizers** and **pesticides** wash off in the rain. This **runoff** makes its way from into rivers and oceans.

nonpoint source pollution—pollution that does not come from one place but many different sources

fertilizer—a substance used to make crops grow better

pesticide—poisonous chemical used to kill insects, rats, and fungi that can damage plants

runoff—water that flows over land instead of soaking into the ground

A farmer treats his crops with a chemical that will kill pests.

..Chemical pollutants cause foamy
scum to wash up on this beach.

FACT

Sometimes nutrients from runoff cause extra algae to grow in the sea. Algae are essential to sea life. Too much algae, however, can be a disaster. Some algae are toxic. They poison the animals that eat them. Others are not toxic, but they require a lot of oxygen from the water. If they use up too much oxygen, other organisms cannot survive.

Nonpoint source pollution contains many chemicals. These chemicals poison sea life, killing them or making them unable to reproduce. This pollution is also harmful to humans. Small organisms and plants absorb elements such as lead and mercury. Small fish eat the organisms and plants. Larger fish eat the smaller fish. Humans eat the larger fish. By this time toxic amounts of lead and mercury have built up in the muscles and organs of the fish. These elements can poison humans.

A Sticky Problem

Most of the world depends on oil as its main source of fuel. Oil is mostly used to make gasoline for transportation. It also runs machinery and is used to make chemicals and plastics.

About one-third of the world's oil comes from the ocean floor. Offshore drilling for oil harms the ocean and the life within it in many ways. The sound waves used to locate oil on the seafloor disrupt ocean life. Whales hear the sound waves and become confused. In some instances, whales beach themselves and die. Also, drilling releases toxic chemicals and substances into the ocean. These can poison ocean life.

FACT

The top 10 oil spills of all time let 940 million gallons (3.6 billion liters) of oil into the sea. That's enough to fill 1,400 Olympic-sized swimming pools.

... an oil rig in the Gulf of Mexico

After it is drilled, oil is transported over the sea. Sometimes the oil is leaked or spilled into the ocean. The impacts of oil spills on marine life and shore birds are devastating. Animals become covered in oil. They inhale or eat the poisonous oil. It irritates their eyes and skin. Many animals are killed instantly.

Gulf of Mexico
Oil Pipe Explosion

The Gulf of Mexico oil spill in 2010 was the worst in U.S. history. This spill was the result of a pipe explosion. An estimated 206 million gallons (780 million liters) of oil leaked into ocean waters. It damaged 16,000 miles (25,750 kilometers) of coastline from Texas to Florida. This spill killed thousands of birds, turtles, and mammals. Some of them were already endangered. This event ranks second in the world's largest oil spills. Some reports state that the oil from this spill is still harming ocean life today.

..a crab covered in oil from a spill

15

Plenty of Fish in the Sea?

In many areas of the world, seafood is a main part of a person's diet. For decades large fishing companies had no limits on how much fish they could catch. The more fish they caught, the more money they could make. But **overfishing** has had a great effect on the ocean. Over the last 70 years, fish have been taken from the ocean faster than they can reproduce. The fishing industry now sees smaller and smaller catches.

overfishing—taking fish from the sea faster than they can reproduce

a large catch of herring in the sea outside of Germany

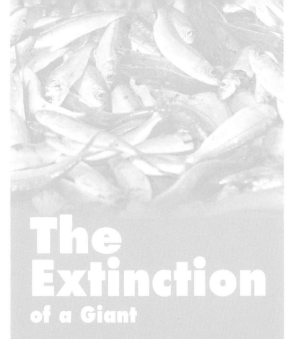

The Extinction
of a Giant

While searching for sea otters, fur hunters sought larger sea animals for food. In 1741 hunters discovered a huge aquatic mammal in Alaskan waters. Steller's sea cow was a cold water relative of manatees and dugongs. Calm, slow-moving, and plentiful, the sea cows were an easy target for hungry fur hunters. In 1768 fur hunters killed the very last one. Just 27 years after it was discovered, Steller's sea cow was extinct.

Many of the fish species commonly caught for food have declined. The Atlantic bluefin tuna population is down to 4 percent of its original numbers. For every 100 of these fish that once dashed through the sea, only four are left.

Overfishing isn't limited to fish. Whales, sea otters, sea turtles, and other marine life can be overfished too. In the 1800s catching whales for meat and oil was a big business. Commercial whaling caused the near extinction of most large whale species. Sea otters were once plentiful in the North Pacific. Hunted for their fur, their numbers dropped to about 2,000 in the early 1900s. The sea otter population has since recovered, and laws now protect them.

Japanese hunted for whales in the Arctic until it was banned in 2014.

Foreign Invaders

Invasive species are plants and animals that move from their habitat into a new one. Sometimes they travel on the hulls of boats. Other times people may bring them to new places. These species can severely damage an ecosystem. They take over the new habitat and take food away from predators local to the area. The whole **food web** can collapse.

.... a diver near a bed of caulerpa

Killer Seaweed!

Even something that seems harmless can become deadly. Caulerpa is green algae native to the Pacific and Indian Oceans. Caulerpa grows fast. It is toxic to most animals. Raised for use in aquariums, it was leaked into the Mediterranean Sea in 1984. Within five years, 11 square feet (1 square meter) had grown to more than 100,000 square feet (9,300 square meters). Soon it appeared on faraway coastlines. It continues to spread, choking out native algae and driving animals away.

.... a Florida manatee

Other Deadly Encounters

Boats are a fun way for many to enjoy the ocean. But boats add another threat for some marine animals. Speeding boats are especially deadly for slow-moving animals such as manatees and sea turtles. The Florida manatee is a mammal that likes to swim in shallow water where it feeds on seagrass. When a fast boat comes near, manatees cannot get out of the way in time.

invasive species — plant or animal that has been artificially introduced into an ecosystem

food web — many food chains connected to one another

FACT

In 2013 boats killed a record 829 manatees in Florida. Only about 5,000 manatees exist near the Florida shores. The 829 that were killed is 16 percent of the Florida manatee population.

19

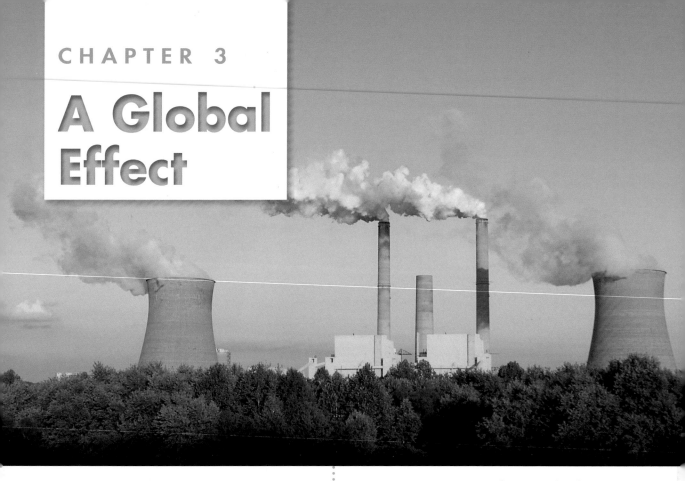

CHAPTER 3
A Global Effect

This power plant burns coal to turn it into electricity. This process releases harmful pollutants into the air.

Ocean life is not the only life in danger. Entire habitats are damaged by human activities. All habitats, land and ocean, are connected. Whatever affects one habitat will in time affect all.

Carbon Dioxide

Carbon dioxide is a gas that animals breathe out. It is also released when burning fuel. Carbon dioxide is in the exhaust of cars and the waste of factories. In the past century, the amount of carbon dioxide in the air has greatly risen. It affects the air and climate. It impacts the sea too.

The extra carbon dioxide in the air reacts with ocean water. It causes the water to have too much acid. The slightest rise in acid can severely harm marine life. The shells of shellfish such as clams and oysters become thin and fragile. Young shellfish will be unable to grow a shell at all. The rise in acidity also makes it harder for corals to produce their sturdy skeletons and to produce young.

a healthy coral reef . . . .

. . . . a reef destroyed by high ocean acidity

Changing Weather

Carbon dioxide causes more harm than just acidic water. Carbon dioxide trapped in the atmosphere creates a **greenhouse effect**. As a result, temperatures around Earth rise. In the ocean, an increase in temperature of just half a degree affects life within. Animals that prefer cold water move closer to the poles. The animals that prey on them must also move to colder waters. If not, they will not get enough to eat.

Another effect of the increase in temperature is melting polar ice. Animals that depend on the polar ice for survival face losing their habitat. Melting ice also means more sea water, which causes the ocean levels to rise and creep higher up shorelines. Millions of animals and people who make their homes on the shores may be forced to move to higher ground. Research shows that sea levels have risen about 0.13 inches (3.2 millimeters) per year for the past 20 years. As temperatures continue to rise, ice will start melting faster. A 3-foot (1-meter) rise in sea level would be disastrous. Low-lying land could become permanently flooded.

FACT

If the entire East Antarctic ice sheet were to melt, it would release enough water to raise sea levels by 164 feet (50 meters).

..... a polar bear on melting ice near the North Pole

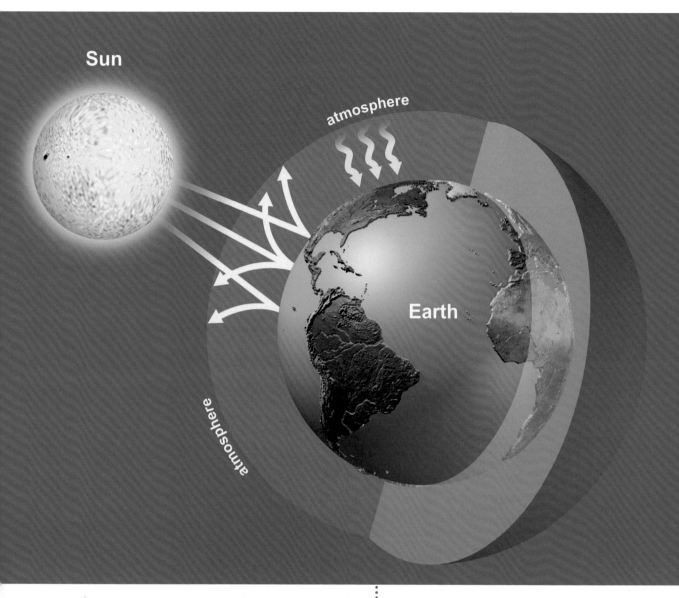

Sun

atmosphere

atmosphere

Earth

The atmosphere helps trap heat to keep Earth warm.

greenhouse effect—warming that happens when certain gases reflect heat toward Earth and make the air warmer

CHAPTER 4

Saving the Seas

Punta Coda Cavallo, a marine protected area near Sardinia, Italy

For all the bad news, there is still plenty of hope. There is a lot of work to do and a lot must change. But if people work together, the seas can once again thrive. What needs to happen to keep Earth's oceans clean and full of life? Scientists have many theories, but most agree on some key steps.

This sea lion, found trapped in a fishing net, was rescued and is being released back into the wild.

Use better fuels.

Scientists are currently learning more about the effects of carbon dioxide on the ocean. But the only real way to stop harm to the ocean is for humans to stop using fuels that release this gas. Humans must find cleaner fuel sources.

Keep pollution out of the ocean.

Industries, organizations, and governments must work together to clean up trash that's already in the ocean to prevent more from entering.

Create more marine protected areas.

These areas protect ocean life and habitats from recreation and fishing. Ocean life is currently thriving in areas of protected ocean, including areas outside of Hawaii and California. If more of these areas are created, ocean life has a better chance of surviving and recovering.

Create better fishing standards and practices.

If people want seafood on the menu in 50 years, at-risk fish must be protected. Fishers need to use practices that protect ecosystems. And the habitat needs to be kept clean and healthy.

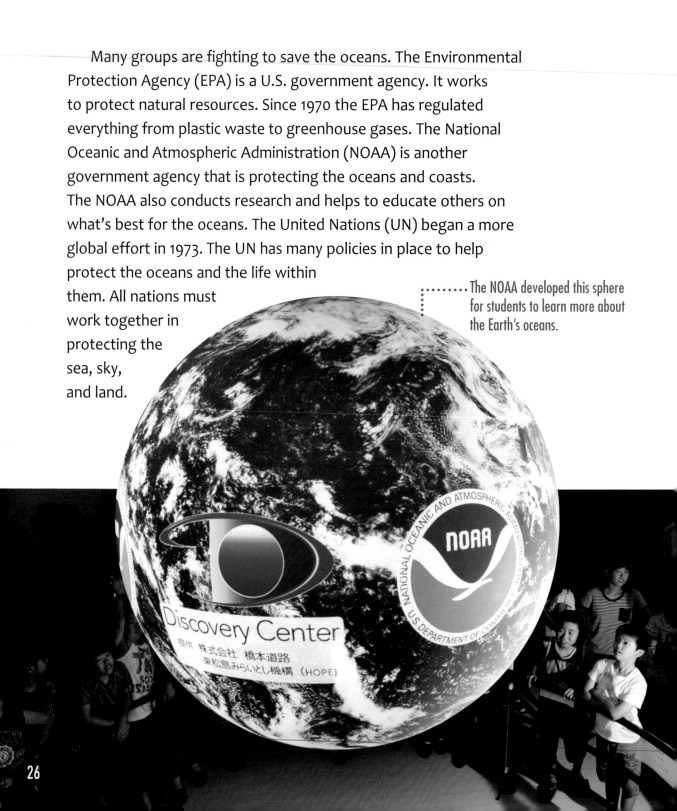

Many groups are fighting to save the oceans. The Environmental Protection Agency (EPA) is a U.S. government agency. It works to protect natural resources. Since 1970 the EPA has regulated everything from plastic waste to greenhouse gases. The National Oceanic and Atmospheric Administration (NOAA) is another government agency that is protecting the oceans and coasts. The NOAA also conducts research and helps to educate others on what's best for the oceans. The United Nations (UN) began a more global effort in 1973. The UN has many policies in place to help protect the oceans and the life within them. All nations must work together in protecting the sea, sky, and land.

The NOAA developed this sphere for students to learn more about the Earth's oceans.

Become Involved

There are many ways ocean lovers can stay connected, even if they don't live near the sea. People can research organizations that benefit the ocean or sea creatures. There are many ways to become involved or raise money. Many conservation efforts have groups anyone can join. They share information about the world's oceans.

Countless nongovernment organizations also work to protect the ocean. The Save Our Seas Foundation and the Ocean Conservancy are just two of the major ones. But it all begins with one person's vision. Anyone can help make a difference.

Environmental workers clean up the shore in Huntington Beach, California.

Think Blue!

Changes must happen around the world in order to keep oceans protected. But everyone can make a difference. These tips will help the everyday person do his or her part in keeping the oceans clean.

Turn off the water.
All the water systems on Earth are connected. Using less water at home helps the oceans.

Reduce, reuse, and recycle.
The process of making disposable items, such as plastics, creates pollution that harms the oceans. Choose options with less packaging. Reuse bags, boxes, and plastic containers. Recycle these items when finished.

Make smart seafood choices.
Seafood lovers can still eat fish and protect the ocean by making educated choices. Shop and pick menu items that are not overfished.

Protect storm drains.
Most gutters lead to storm drains. Many storm drains lead to the ocean. Find safe ways to dispose of soap, paint, or other harmful chemicals.

Bike or walk.

Most vehicles run on gasoline, which harms air that eventually reaches the ocean. By using less gas and oil, fewer ocean-harming substances are released into the air.

The oceans are endangered, but not gone. There's time to turn things around. People caused the problems, but people can fix them.

29

Glossary

aquaculture (ah-kwa-CALL-chur)—raising aquatic animals in water for human use

current (KUHR-uhnt)—the movement of water in a river or an ocean

equator (i-KWAY-tuhr)—an imaginary line around the middle of Earth

evaporate (i-VA-puh-rayt)—to change from a liquid into a vapor or a gas

fertilizer (FUHR-tuh-ly-zuhr)—a substance used to make crops grow better

food web (FEWD WEB)—many food chains connected to one another

fossil fuels (FAH-suhl FYOOLZ)—fuels, including coal, oil, or natural gas, made from the remains of ancient organisms

greenhouse effect (GREEN-houss uh-FEKT)—warming that happens when certain gases reflect heat toward Earth and make the air warmer

habitat (HAB-uh-tat)—the natural place and conditions in which a plant or animal lives

hydroelectric (hye-droh-i-LEK-trik)—to do with the production of electricity from moving water

invasive species (in-VAY-siv SPEE-sheez)—plant or animal that has been artificially introduced into an ecosystem

nonpoint source pollution (non-POINT SORSS puh-LOO-shuhn)—pollution that does not come from one place but many different sources

overfishing (OH-vur-FISH-ing)—taking fish from the sea faster than they can reproduce

pesticide (pess-TI-side)—poisonous chemical used to kill insects, rats, and fungi that can damage plants

phytoplankton (FITE-oh-plangk-tuhn)—different kinds of one-celled organisms that live in water and provide food for larger creatures

pollution (puh-LOO-shuhn)—harmful materials that damage the air, water, and soil

runoff (ruhn-AWF)—water that flows over land instead of soaking into the ground

Critical Thinking Using the Common Core

1. How have humans harmed the ocean? Use evidence from the text to support your answer. (Key Idea and Details)

2. Reread the paragraph on page 8 about hydroelectric power. Then reread Chapter 3 (pages 20–23). How would Earth be different if hydroelectric power was the main source of fuel for humans? (Integration of Knowledge and Ideas)

3. Compare and contrast the two photos on pages 21. How have changes in the ocean water affected coral reefs? (Craft and Structure)

Read More

Allgor, Marie. *Endangered Ocean Animals*. Save Earth's Animals! New York: PowerKids Press, 2013.

Jakubiak, David J. *What Can We Do About Oil Spills and Ocean Pollution?* Protecting Our Planet. New York: PowerKids Press, 2012.

Mulder, Michelle. *Every Last Drop: Bringing Clean Water Home*. Orca Footprints. Custer, Wash.: Orca Book Publishers, 2014.

Newman, Patricia. *Plastic, Ahoy! Investigating the Great Pacific Garbage Patch*. Minneapolis: Millbrook Press, 2014.

Internet Sites

FactHound offers a safe, fun way to find Internet sites related to this book. All of the sites on FactHound have been researched by our staff.

Here's all you do:

Visit *www.facthound.com*

Type in this code: 9781491420386

Super-cool stuff!

Check out projects, games and lots more at
www.capstonekids.com

Index